HOW TO NAVIGATE YOUR CAREER LIKE A LEGEND

HOW TO NAVIGATE YOUR CAREER LIKE A LEGEND

Natalie Abou-Alwan

BROWN
DOG
BOOKS

Published under licence by Brown Dog Books and
The Self-Publishing Partnership Ltd, 10b Greenway Farm, Bath Rd,
Wick, nr. Bath BS30 5RL, UK

www.selfpublishingpartnership.co.uk

ISBN printed book: 978-1-83952-953-5
ISBN e-book: 978-1-83952-954-2

Cover design by Kevin Rylands
Internal design by Matthew Blurton
Internal illustrations © by Natalie Abou-Alwan

Printed and bound in the UK

This book is printed on FSC® certified paper

MIX
Paper | Supporting
responsible forestry
FSC
www.fsc.org   FSC® C013604

For my father, my mother and my sister.
Thank you for teaching me how to love purely,
how to live by integrity
and how to build resilience.

CONTENTS

Introduction

THE WHY

I am not a trained writer. I am a lawyer. A working professional who, probably like you, has observed the general goings-on in the office, across boardroom tables and during commercial negotiations, at home and abroad.

I have been managed and I have managed. I have been led and I have led. I have been mentored and I have mentored. I have been inspired by truly magnetic individuals and I have been appalled by the bad behaviour of those who really should know better.

I have worked through the night and over weekends and cancelled holidays to meet reduced deadlines (ok, the latter just the once, but still). I have given my all and my full loyalty to each organisation for which I have worked. I continue to do so, but with a wiser head and an increasingly confident core.

You might be a seasoned employee, rising through the ranks, or maybe you are starting your career adventure fresh out of school, college or university.

If you are experiencing difficulties in the workplace – perhaps you are dealing with tricky individuals, a toxic work environment, or the fear or even hatred of the dreaded networking, to name just a few – then this companion is for you.

I sincerely hope that by using this companion, you will feel less alone and more aware of the game that is being played by others.

Most importantly, though, I hope that my experiences over the past 25 years may help to empower you to navigate your particular situation by providing some useful tips and suggestions, so that you can start to feel more confident in yourself and really push your career as far forward as you desire. Unashamedly and unapologetically.

Wishing each and every one of you your most successful steps ahead!

Chapter One

"CHECK YOUR EGO AT THE DOOR"

CHECK YOUR EGO AT THE DOOR....

These were the words written by Quincy Jones in felt-tip capitals and taped to the door of the A&M Recording Studios in Hollywood on the night of 28 January 1985. Forty-six of the brightest stars of that time in the American music industry were soon to walk through these doors and spend a solid, unrelenting ten hours recording the anthem "We Are The World", written only days before by Michael Jackson and Lionel Richie.

A recent documentary on Netflix reminds us that what makes this night even more remarkable is that most of the artists found their way to the studios immediately after attending the American Music Awards held at the Shrine Auditorium in Los Angeles at which, incidentally, its host for the evening, Lionel Richie, scooped six awards. Alongside him, the likes of Cyndi Lauper, Tina Turner, Willie Nelson and Kenny Rogers, also winners at the event, rushed over to the A&M Recording Studios, rather than celebrating their accomplishments at after-show parties. No doubt it crossed their minds that they were about to attend the party of their life among fellow musical talents and living legends, including Ray Charles, Smokey Robinson, Diana Ross, Stevie Wonder, Huey Lewis, Bruce Springsteen, Dionne Warwick and Bob Dylan.

The pressure (and under the studio lights, the heat) was on to record blended choruses and solo sections throughout the night and into the early hours of the morning, with all the artists in the same room, rehearsing and finding their pitch in front of one another.

Quincy Jones had literally no time for inflated self-opinions, discord, diva-esque behaviour, nor tantrums. Sure, there were moments of nerves and even debates about what language the lyrics should be rendered in (Stevie Wonder suggesting the inclusion of a line in Swahili at one stage), but with the smooth assistance of Lionel Richie as pacifier, Stevie Wonder as voice coach and Quincy

Jones as a gracious master of ceremonies, the song was recorded in perpetuity for millions to enjoy all around the world.

That night, egos were very much checked at the door, for these reasons: (i) Quincy Jones had requested their presence; (ii) they were in the aura of their very own musical heroes (swapping autographs for each other on copies of their own music sheets); and (iii) they knew they were there for a greater cause. The record, inspired by Bob Geldof's Live Aid, was intended to raise funds in the hope of reducing poverty and famine in Africa. Egos were not required.

I have often been struck by the lack of egotism shown by those whom one might usually expect to carry this rather flashy and crude mantel. Like many of you, I have worked on intense deals, mostly throughout the night and sometimes into the next afternoon, where much is required to be achieved in a relatively short space of time, and regularly across various time zones.

One such deal immediately springs to mind, where the timetable to reach completion was shockingly tight. Several flights to differing geographical locations, locked in banking or law firm offices for over 12 hours each day, re-scheduling holidays to accommodate various deal milestones, and endless cups of strong coffee and hurriedly prepared sandwiches all contributed to a gruelling and exhausting set of weeks. However, what shone bright for me throughout this time was the gratitude and appreciation demonstrated by the commercial deal team leader. He was there at the coalface, constantly. Day and night. Never expecting his team to work harder or longer than he did.

I particularly remember picking up his phone call, at 3 am London time, from a remote location he was required to fly to as part of the deal-closing process. "I hate to ask you to do this, I know you have hardly slept over the past few weeks, but I really need your help on this one" rang down the scratchy phone line, emphasising just how remote his location was. He already knew I would be awake: I was amending a set of documents which needed to be turned around overnight and I had been exchanging emails with the team over the past few hours. His request would add to my to-do list that night, but this was urgent.

Why give so much to this deal? Why answer the phone at 3 am? Why add to an already expanding workload?

For me, it was simple. As an in-house lawyer, I was there to support my commercial colleagues through thick and thin. Had this been the norm, or even a very regular scenario, I think it would quite quickly and easily have lost its appeal. Yet this was not the case. At that time, the deal itself was ground-breaking for many reasons and I was working with intelligent, experienced and driven individuals, from whom I learned a great amount. Not to mention that they each had a good sense of humour, a crucial quality in these types of tense circumstances. We were truly working together, as one team, for a common cause. Perhaps not quite in the philanthropic realms of the intentions behind "We Are The World", but definitely just as relentlessly and with as much energy and precision required to get the deal done as accurately and professionally as possible, in the time given. No egos were required, nor invited into that equivalent of a studio and I truly believe this was one of the main reasons we were able to close the deal so efficiently and successfully.

"Every day, my daddy told me the same thing. 'Once a task is just begun, never leave it till it's done. Be the labour great or small, do it well or not at all.'" I couldn't agree more, Quincy Jones.

Journal

Journal

_____

_____

_____

_____

_____

_____

_____

_____

_____

_____

_____

_____

_____

_____

_____

_____

_____

_____

_____

_____

_____

_____

_____

Chapter 2

ONE BAD APPLE

There's always one, isn't there?

As our careers develop, we will all have had plenty of experience working in, or with, various teams. Some of these experiences will have had a very positive impact, others less so. There will be multiple reasons for this, however one that I have noticed time and again is that it takes just one bad apple to spoil the whole bunch. Here's what I mean.

Imagine for a moment that you are working in a prestigious office, with interesting work and surrounded by colleagues who are of all ages, all creeds, happily working well with one another. Then along comes the big bad wolf. An individual so out of tune with their surroundings, so oblivious to the impact they are having on their fellow workers and so lacking in self-awareness that outside of the rulebook on diversity, equity and inclusion it would be comical. But it is not comical. Several individuals in the team have already been caught crying as they withstand verbal blows, angry with themselves for getting emotional, but in the circumstances there seem to be few other options. No concerns are raised, no reprimands are issued and, you've guessed it, the abuse is allowed to continue. Bottom line: team morale decreases, and so does performance.

Many of you will already be aware that the Equality Act 2010 states that employers are liable for harassment of any type in the workplace. Malicious gossip is included. According to a September 2024 report by the CIPD (Chartered Institute of Personnel and Development) a quarter of employees in the UK experienced conflict or abuse in the workplace.

I, too, have found myself in a situation where just one more verbal punch, dealt in a calculated, stealthy and cold fashion, forced me to break my masked composure, feeling my eyes fill with tears of shock, frustration and sheer exhaustion. There is no other word for it: this is adult bullying in the workplace.

I could devote a whole chapter to leaders who are bullies: not to those above them (quite the contrary, it would appear), but to targeted individuals within their teams they are nothing short of professionally lethal. Instead, I would like to focus here on leaders who have a bully in their team. How can you ensure that this is dealt with quickly, effectively and professionally?

Put simply, know your team. Below are a few suggestions for how you might go about this.

Firstly, observe. Really watch your team – and I don't mean in a creepy, clandestine way, but rather as an outsider would. Pay attention to how the team interacts, not just in meetings, which can in themselves feel like a performance, but also in more casual settings: at the coffee machine, in the corridors, at their desks. Does the team atmosphere change for the better when a specific individual is absent for one reason or another?

Secondly, listen. Here, meetings are often a good starting-point. Is there one individual who is more dominating, who says things apparently meant in jest, which to a more sensitive colleague could feel more like an insult? Another clue may be found in the person in your team who is constantly in your ear. Relaying "stories" about certain individuals and providing you with their opinion in a manipulative way, in other words by making you think it was your idea in the first place, and that they are simply corroborating this with each and every mouthful of gossip.

Thirdly, ensure your team knows you have their back. This is paramount. Letting them know you are there to support and improve their daily experience is so important, allowing a solid pipeline of open communication to be established. This will help to develop a two-way stream of dialogue, and ultimately of trust, in which an employee being bullied, or a bystander, feels they can raise with you their experience and the negative impact it is having on them, or on their fellow teammate.

Fourthly, explore. We should all be putting in time with each of our team members, but how many of us really use this time to delve a little deeper? By this I don't mean getting inappropriately personal, but instead allowing that individual space and freedom to open up about how they are truly feeling. For example, have they seemed a little withdrawn, lacking in energy and motivation, or do they seem more nervous, anxious or less confident when a certain individual is present?

Finally, acknowledge that you are not always right! Bullies can be incredibly charming and may seem completely trustworthy to the person they want to convince. This is their key skill. They are ruthless and will play the right role to the right person at the right time. They often want you to believe that your team couldn't function without them. Check yourself for any signs of bias, especially if that individual is a high performer. This should be irrelevant in dealing with the issue at hand.

Now, how best to tackle the bully? After taking actions similar to those outlined above, there is only one thing left to do. Confront the bully.

As we know, it is difficult to argue with facts, so having detailed episodes and observations to hand will be incredibly helpful. Remember, hearsay is difficult to prove, which is why your observations will be vital. Ask them what their intentions were in certain scenarios and whether they can appreciate the impact their actions might have on others. Give them a set amount of time to reflect and course-correct themselves, making it clear that the continuation of certain behaviours will just not be tolerated. Ensure you continue to observe the team's general mood and any positive changes. Put in place a reliable coach or mentor relationship to work with the individual, to ensure that constructive change can be given a chance. If needs be, work with HR through more formal routes to bolster any further course-correction required. If all else fails, it may be time to consider other options, including dismissal.

As a leader, it is your duty to protect your team, to allow them to flourish in a safe environment.

Archbishop Desmond Tutu summed it up succinctly: *"If you are neutral in situations of injustice, you have chosen the side of the oppressor."*

Journal

Journal

Chapter 3

THE FEMALE OF THE SPECIES IS MORE DEADLY THAN THE MALE

don't know about you, but I have often wondered whether this is a universal truth. After all, history and literature remind us that a woman scorned is something to be feared, particularly if you are on the receiving end of her contempt. I accept that the sisterhood does exist. Like many of you, I have felt its inspiring and powerful engine, but it is certainly not the norm, and surprisingly sparse just where you might expect it to be most prevalent. I have often asked myself why. After years of observation and direct experience, I feel that I am able to shed some light on this taboo subject.

We have all heard the stories of women in corporate settings whose voices are suppressed by their alpha male counterpart, who is more than likely earning a higher wage for doing the same job, often with less experience than the female, but with more bravado and a stronger network to tip that balance. The more women I speak to across industries, the more I recognise their experience of being abused, yet not by their male colleague flexing his muscles (often literally), instead – more shockingly – by a female in power. A female whose tactics are more subtle (at least to men), but potentially far more ruthless and damaging to one of her own species.

I entered the corporate world in the late 1990s, post the Dynasty-shoulder-padded female executive zenith, yet I was constantly being reminded of the great debt owed by me and others in my position to the Pankhurstian Boadiceas of the legal profession, who selflessly blazed a trail for us softer and weaker fledglings embarking on our careers. We were to look up to these female fortresses and gaze in awe at their relentless fight to pave the way for those who came after them. I have no problem with this as a concept. Many of these women were indeed brave in blazing the trail, and their sacrifices and achievements are undeniable. However, disappointingly, in many cases these fortresses were buttressed so tightly, with all drawbridges firmly lifted and locked in place, that any newcomer had no hope of crossing the moat of knowledge, nor of scaling the towers of experience: "Admire us from afar, fear us even, but stay where you are. We have climbed the ladder, good for us, and don't you dare expect us to lower it down for you."

You know as well as I do that this is the absolute antithesis of sisterhood, and yet a bit like the menopause: whilst experienced by many women, it is surprisingly little talked about. So why is this common experience not more widely aired? One theory is the concern that raising these issues openly might lead to women living up to the "gossipy/bitchy" stereotype, which some would say has been perpetrated mainly by men. Another theory plays out more like a Clint Eastwood Spaghetti-Western movie, the feeling that when it comes to corporate quotas for women in power, "this town ain't big enough for the both of us". Indeed, a recent MSCI report[1] found that while boards with female representation of at least 30% successfully achieved cumulative returns 18.9% higher than those without such representation, a majority percentage of board committees across markets still had no female director representation whatsoever.

And while paying lip service to the importance of diversity, equity and inclusion, why are so many women in power simultaneously putting so much of their energy into pushing others down, while lifting themselves higher? I agree that it is not just women who should be helping other women to pursue their full career potential, but they do seem to be a relatively obvious place to start.

I am certainly no psychologist, but it doesn't take a professional to recognise that one of the causes at the core of this behaviour is insecurity. Distilled, the key lies in fear, pure and simple: in some

---

1. MSCI Women on Boards and Beyond report 2024.

cases it triggers a deep-rooted lack of self-worth, perhaps even a strong self-loathing; in others it provokes a decision (conscious or not) to take on the behaviour of male colleagues to remain in power. For these women their careers are, in their minds only, often the only achievement they have managed, to neutralise the impact of the school bully, the disappointing exam result, the neglectful or harsh parent, the wayward husband or the physical self-criticism playing like an old VHS video in their head.

What can we do to change this behaviour and bring down those drawbridges? Expecting others to change requires a recognition of the problem and a willingness to do things differently. Many of these women are already too exhausted, expending their energy on networking upwards, to have leftover oxygen to stop, breathe and reflect on the damage they may be leaving in their wake. We therefore cannot solely rely on change at this level. Rather, it is down to the true sisterhood to ensure that they continue to act as the antidote, the vaccine if you like, in this day and age and encourage immunity among the female population at the receiving end of this behaviour, allowing talent to flourish.

It takes courage and self-belief to ensure that these bad examples do not wound and scar, but rather act as a lesson: "This is not the way I will behave towards others". Only then can we allow ourselves the hope that change is coming, loud and clear.

If only I could put my arm around my fledgling self, what advice would I give her? Here are my top tips on how to navigate similar experiences, in the hope that we can start to break the cycle of bad behaviour:

- "It's not me, it's you" – especially early on in your career, it is not easy to shut off the noise, take a step back and see the situation for what it really is: the "Queen Bee syndrome". I found that working hard and focussing on the job in hand helped me not only to build my knowledge and experience, but also my confidence – acting as my own fortress if you like – which became better equipped to repel the arrows.

- "Seek wise counsel" – actively seek feedback from those whom you trust and respect in the workplace, either clients or colleagues. This will help to rebalance the lack of support and negativity, acting as a counter to any inbuilt self-criticism.
- "Nobody's perfect" – if you are receiving consistent messages in your feedback from both Queen Bee and those whom you trust, use this constructively as an opportunity to work on those concerns. This will take the issue out of the spotlight and will serve to make you a better, more rounded and thoughtful professional.
- "Shake it off" – as Taylor Swift would say. I have often wondered why women in general tend to hold on to and internalise criticism, whereas men seem to find it easier to let go, taking it less personally. If you can, try to stay objective and keep focussed on your goals, which will push Queen Bee out of your limelight.
- "Role model" – whether real or fictional, I sometimes imagine how someone I am impressed with would handle a particular situation. I have found that it can help as a source of strength and inspiration.
- "Make a break for freedom" – if all else fails and your workday continues to resemble a scene out of *The Devil Wears Prada*, remember that you hold the controls and you can decide when it's time to switch channels. Working with good recruitment firms will help you polish your CV and allow you to realise your worth in the market.

I will leave you with a couple of thoughts. Firstly, my sincere gratitude to those women in powerful positions who actively help to pull talented females up with them, who have gone the extra mile to encourage and support women during the highs and lows of their careers and who are the true warriors, breaking barriers, stereotypes and the bad behaviour of some of their species (please see the next chapter, "Why We Need More Marilyn Monroes", to read more about these Boadiceas).

Finally, as Eleanor Roosevelt once said: ***"No one can make you feel inferior without your consent."***

Journal

Journal

Chapter 4

WHY WE NEED MORE MARILYN MONROES

f it's ok with you, let me start by sharing a true story about one of my favourite American idols, Marilyn Monroe – and please bear with me if you are not (yet) a Marilyn fan.

It is 15 March 1955 in Los Angeles, almost a decade before President Lyndon B. Johnson took steps to abolish segregation in the United States through the Civil Rights Act. Black singers were banned from singing in certain nightclubs, such as the Mocambo on Sunset Boulevard, West Hollywood, a club frequented by Hollywood greats such as Clark Gable, Elizabeth Taylor and Marlene Dietrich. This was where Frank Sinatra made his début as a solo performer in 1943 and where Marilyn Monroe, like many of her peers, chose to kick back and relax to the sounds of the biggest acts of the moment. In fact, rather than me telling you the story, here it is in the words of the great Ella Fitzgerald, who was on the receiving end of Marilyn's support:

"I owe Marilyn Monroe a real debt … she personally called the owner of the Mocambo and told him she wanted me booked immediately, and if he would do it, she would take a front table every night… She told him – and it was true, due to Marilyn's superstar status – that the press would go wild. The owner said yes, and Marilyn was there, front table, every night. The press went overboard. After that, I never had to play a small jazz club again. She was an unusual woman – a little ahead of her times. And she didn't know it."

What had Marilyn Monroe to gain from putting her neck on the line for a lesser-known female artist? At that time, Marilyn was fast rising to the top of the motion picture industry, with a list of hit movies under her belt (or taffeta sash, whichever you prefer) and a surging fan base, despite her recent divorce from her superhero ex-husband, the much-lauded New York Yankees baseball player,

Joe DiMaggio. The answer is nothing. Absolutely nothing, except joy in helping to promote the talent she so clearly identified in this shy jazz singer, who went on to be known as the Queen of Jazz and the First Lady of Song.

Having read quite a bit about Marilyn Monroe and her struggle to be treated as a serious actress, instead of a blonde bimbo, I believe that alongside the joy she experienced in helping others there was also a strong sense of equality and fairness. She herself felt misunderstood, mistreated and quite frankly abused. So rather than expecting others to have to withstand the same fate, she instead extended a manicured hand to those who she could see were struggling with similar horrors which she herself knew only too well. The fact that, by law, singers such as Ella Fitzgerald were routinely denied access to quite literally the "white club", which was the playing-field for artists in this case and was from the outset grossly uneven, to put it mildly. Marilyn spotted the talent and the inequality, and she did something about it. By opening up this one opportunity to Ella, Marilyn created a springboard from which the First Lady of Song rocketed into the history books of music and modern culture, not only in her home country of the United States but also around the world and for decades to come.

I shall now move on from 1955 into the 1990s. I was at a boarding school in Kent, in the second year of my A-levels and deliberating about my UCCA form (Universities Central Council on Admissions, as it was then known). I was aiming high, but uncertain of whether I might make it into the ivory towers of Oxbridge. Several teachers tried to dissuade me: "University isn't for everyone Natalie" and "You won't get over the rejection" were the words I heard before I had even put pen to paper and filled in "University of Oxford" on my form. I heard their words, but I chose not to listen. They were not going to hold me back, but I needed encouragement. So I sought out one teacher in particular who had always inspired me to do better and believe in myself. She seemed to see a spark of potential in me from a relatively early age and I would need her help now. I rushed up to the teachers' study, knocked politely on the door and requested a quick word with Miss Boyce. Out she came and I blurted out: "I want to apply for Oxford. Mr X and Miss Y have told me not to. Do you think I can do it?" I felt that my future was hanging on her answer. She looked at me with every piece of assurance I needed and said: "Yes. You can do it." Well, that was it. Out came the black biro and off went my UCCA form in the post that very day. Miss Boyce opened the door of opportunity for me. She believed in me, she dealt the cards, we placed our chips and now all I had to do was win the hand. I did win the hand and I shall always be grateful for her support.

Fast forward a little further and we are in 2015. While my career as an in-house lawyer was developing and I was advising the heads of business and risk in my own industry, I was keen to grow further and gain more experience right at the strategic core of the decision-making process in other industries too. I started to look at board positions which I sensed might fulfil these developmental cravings in me. I researched about how to be a NED (non-executive director), attended various evening sessions teaching the ins and outs of how to navigate a set of accounts and financial statements, searched online for board vacancies and applied for a handful of these. Nothing. Then something amazing happened. I was at a corporate event in one of London's swankiest hotels, sitting in a break-out session where we were discussing how to get more women onto boards. A shimmer of aquamarine light caught my eye. It hung majestically around the neck of a fellow attendee. Not only was she a very successful lawyer and multiple board member, she was also a jewellery designer and this necklace was one of her own stunning creations. We hit it off immediately and I continue to seek her wise counsel on many dilemmas. At one of these meetups, she said, "I have been approached for a board position. They specifically want a lawyer, but my various obligations at the moment mean that I don't think I would be able to devote the time that I would otherwise like to. Would you mind if I recommend you? I think they would be very lucky to have you." Would I mind? I was ready to bite her hand off! She had identified potential in me and opened the door to an opportunity I would not otherwise have had.

I spent several enlightening years on that board, learning and developing my skills in a different industry from the one that was in my comfort zone, but most of all I continue to be so grateful to countless successful women like this who spot potential in other women and put their necks on the line for them. There are so many women I could name in my own career, but the word-count won't allow me to include them all. The irony is that these women probably wouldn't even know that this chapter is about them, including the woman who encouraged me to start writing about my professional experiences in the first place. They do not help in order to be thanked, or for praise or recognition. They help for the mere joy of it and, I firmly believe, to help level out that playing field.

A huge thank you to all of you women from all the women who, like me, have benefitted from your encouragement, support and empathy. You have recognised the light inside us and kept it nurtured to glow even brighter.

I rather like these encouraging words from Marilyn Monroe herself: ***"We are all of us stars, and we deserve to twinkle."***

Journal

Journal

Chapter 5

TO WORK OR TO NETWORK?

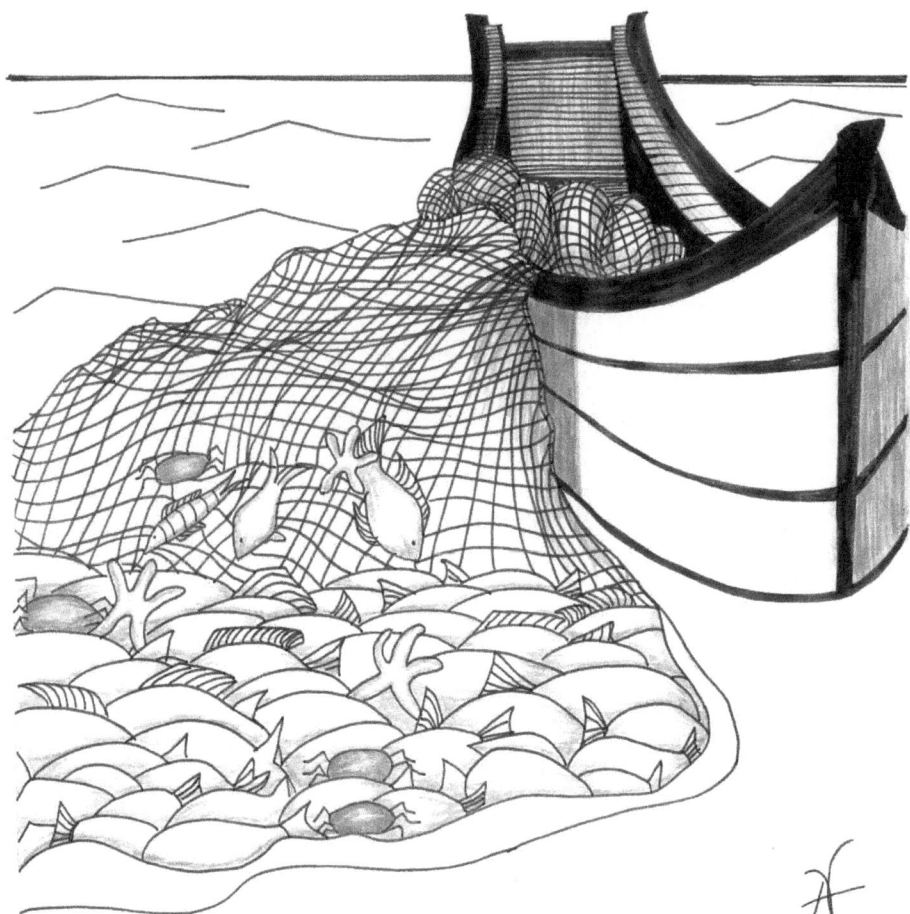

"How on earth did X get the job?" – I wonder how many times you have heard this or thought this yourself about a colleague? Was it through sheer hard graft or was it down to something else? If it was something else, what was that something else?

In my experience, there are three types of worker looking to achieve professional success:

1. Those who believe that just by getting your head down and working hard, your efforts will be rewarded on merit;
2. Others who believe that by putting less focus on work and more focus on networking, success will be inevitable; and
3. A third category who believe something in the middle: hard work is needed, but this needs to be balanced with significant time dedicated to networking.

Which one are you?

I hate to say it, but I spent most of my career believing in the principle of worker number 1 above. Surely if I just worked hard, gained experience and received strong feedback from my peers and clients, then success would come calling. Right? I think we all know the answer. What a fool I was!

Don't get me wrong: hard work is important, especially in the early part of your career as you absorb information, learn the nuts and bolts of your particular industry, make mistakes and learn from them. Hard work should continue, too, as you grow and take on more responsibilities, perhaps start managing a team and gain wider accountabilities. But around this juncture something changes and the lanes seem to split into two (I know I am simplifying here, but no doubt you get the point): one lane for the meteoric risers and the other for the rest.

Why does this happen, and who picks the meteors? I have witnessed time and again a certain "type" that hits the fast lane. So, what are they doing that the rest are not? The answer usually rests on one activity: networking.

Like many of you, I have mentored men and women, both within my own workplace and outside of it. I have co-chaired an ethnic minorities network, made up of approximately 1,000 employees in one of these workplaces and I have done quite a lot of work across minority groups. Something that really stood out to me was the gulf that seems to exist between the majority group and the minorities, particularly in this area of networking.

Speaking to many employees, I realised that most of those in the minority categories and, more often than not, ethnic minorities (both male and female) were simply not brought up to network and were not taught the seeming importance of this in the workplace. Their parents would instil this dictum into them at a young age: "Keep your head down at work, don't stand out, work hard and be grateful for the job you have." In fact, in some cultures, being deferential to one's boss and peers, even when you disagree with them on an issue, is the only way to behave. Anything else would cause you to raise your head above the parapet and make waves where you shouldn't and bottom line, it would be considered downright offensive.

Similarly, I often hear others, usually women, saying: "I just feel awkward putting time into someone's diary to talk about myself, especially when they are very senior and busy." Whilst at the same time, the men I mentor have already chatted to Mr or Ms Important at the coffee machine, discussed the football results or their families, and agreed to join their group for a quick drink after work that evening.

This chasm of behaviour therefore puts minority groups at another disadvantage in the workplace. So, how can we change this? I think the first step is awareness of the issue and from that should come a commitment to adjust environments and measurements for success to be truly inclusive. I am sure we have all read the various industry and academic reports which resoundingly highlight the importance of diversity to a corporation's profitability, but it is the concept of inclusivity that is more fundamental and therefore much harder to tackle successfully. Alongside this, more effort is needed from the individual employee to build their confidence and ease in "socialising" more within the workplace. I don't believe you can have one without the other, so it really is a pincer movement, a 'top-down' and 'bottom-up' approach.

Here are just a few suggestions around how you might start to re-think your concerns about networking:

- **Don't think of it as networking!** – the word "networking" itself can send shivers down some people's spines. Rather than perceive it as false and 'time-wasting', perhaps try to think of it from the opposite perspective. You are not getting to know somebody: instead, they are getting to know you. Psychologically, this can take the emphasis off you actively "time-wasting" and feeling awkward about doing it. Instead, it shifts it to a more positive experience, allowing the other person to start to understand you better. As we all know, we usually have more in common with others than we think, but we only learn this when we start to communicate.
- **Mitigate the risk of being left behind** – we all have different drivers and motivations in the workplace, and that is a good thing. However, if what you want is concrete

progression in your career, you will need to pull out of the same lane and move across to the next one. This requires getting your name out there and one of the ways to achieve this is by speaking to a wider net of people. When I started to do this, I noticed that more opportunities came my way just through a short conversation with someone in a different area/location/discipline, perhaps using a recent piece of work as an icebreaker, which can also showcase your achievements.

- **Seek out a mentor you trust** – do not be afraid to make direct contact with someone who inspires you and from whom you feel you could learn. Ask them if they would be interested in mentoring you. From a human perspective, not only is this extremely flattering for them, but it should also help you work through any particular concerns you are facing at the time. Strong mentorship usually leads to strong sponsorship (from a person in power who will advocate for you) and this is key to your progression.

As mentioned, it is not just down to the individual who is already reluctant to "put themselves out there". Corporations, too, have a part to play in this and below are just a couple of examples that I have seen work successfully.

- **Recognise networking as a career accelerator** – organisations need to openly acknowledge this and therefore recognise that minority groups need more encouragement and support in building their networks.
- **Focus on inclusivity** – this really is the hardest part, but it is vital. If your organisation does not foster an authentic

environment where each employee feels welcomed and, most importantly, equal, then how are employees going to feel part of the larger picture and comfortable enough to speak out? Ignoring this means ignoring your best asset: your talent and, ultimately, your potential future as a profitable and successful company.

- **Create a level playing-field** – this can be done from the initial job specification stage, straight through to how success is measured in both performance reviews and promotions.
- **Seek out the quietest voice** – and listen to it! Each employee has something of value to offer, so make sure you create the space to harness this, rather than lose it in the wider noise.

I appreciate that this is a huge topic to cover in a short chapter and we will all have so much more to add here, but if I can leave you with one thought on this, it would be that: we all have a place in this world, so do not be afraid to spread your net wide!

Journal

Journal

Chapter 6

"I'M NOT YOUR BOSS, I'M YOUR BROTHER"

stelle Brown walked into a rehearsal room in Las Vegas. It was a hot July day in 1969. Plenty of expectation hung in the desert air on this first day of rehearsals for a new live show. The audience had been waiting nine years for this epic moment. Elvis Presley appeared with his usual grandeur, walked over to Estelle and her group, The Sweet Inspirations, also made up of Cissy Houston (mother of Whitney Houston) and introduced himself: "Hey ladies, I'm Elvis Presley." As though they or anyone else on the planet at the time didn't know!

The Sweet Inspirations performed as Elvis' backing singers for eight years, up until his untimely death in 1977, leaving their homes and families for six-week stints, twice a year, with two sell-out shows every night. They were performing with the King of Rock 'n' Roll, a musical phenomenon, who blasted through boundaries established by "white folk" to separate them from those whose skin colour was deeper than theirs. This was Memphis, Tennessee in the 1950s. Radio listeners identified the voice as belonging to a white man when a local disc jockey revealed the name of his school (only white children were allowed to enrol in Humes High School) and they couldn't believe their ears.

In 1969, the pressure was on to deliver, not just for Elvis, but also for The Sweet Inspirations and the rest of Elvis' hand-picked band and deliver is what they did. Night after night. Estelle and her fellow backing singers could easily have broken free, given up on the pressure and intensity of these performances, these long periods away from their home comforts, but something kept them there and it wasn't the money. Estelle explained why many years later. Her impulse was always to call the King of Rock 'n' Roll, "Boss". After all, he directed them and expected them to perform to the best of their abilities, yet he also benefitted from their time and talent and ultimately, he paid their wages. But Elvis was having none of this. His response to Estelle was simply: "I'm not your boss, I'm your brother." As Estelle recalled: "He didn't put himself above. We were on the same level." Elvis didn't need to elevate himself, he *was* the boss, but it was the authentic way in which he led his band members and how he made them feel that ensured their continued loyalty to him. The Sweet Inspirations respected and trusted their "brother", a white man reciprocating their respect and trust, who quite literally catapulted them onto the big stage with him. That is why they continued to perform alongside the King.

I feel that this concept of a trusted individual in a position of authority who provides someone else with a stage or platform, without using that position of authority to overwhelm or denigrate that someone else, is truly inspiring and unequivocally authentic. It is these individuals who lead by example, either consciously or unconsciously writing a new rule book which those whom they have taken the time to help and encourage will read and practise, ensuring that these actions form golden threads which grow stronger and endure.

Although I have written about the impact of women in the workplace, I would like to focus here on men in the workplace, in particular those in powerful positions, who detect talent in women and actively choose to draw this out and encourage their voice to be heard. Whether this is demonstrating genuine empathy for career disappointments and helping them to overcome these, or openly sponsoring them within the organisation, or revealing their own networks, both within the industry and outside of it. I have experienced all of these examples from powerful men during my career. Let me share some of them with you.

On a wintry December evening many years ago, the entire department of several hundred employees was invited to a

Christmas dinner in central London. This really was the last thing I felt like doing. A couple of days earlier, I had been devastated by the news that a less experienced male, but one who had been at the company longer than me and with a stronger network (read more on networks in the "To Work or to Network" chapter), would be my new manager. This was a position I had prepared and interviewed for, with the encouragement and full backing of various key business stakeholders. Although I am relatively small in stature, that evening I certainly wasn't standing tall and proud. We were asked to take our seats and I felt as though I didn't belong, and frankly I didn't want to be there. Moments later, in these bleak surroundings, I felt a hand on my shoulder. "I am so glad you came. How are you doing?" were the words I heard, my eyes still fixed on the wooden table I was sitting at. I looked up and standing next to me was the organisation's Group General Counsel, Rupert Bondy. The head honcho. I tried to respond, but my emotions got the better of me. Instead of speaking, I choked and could feel the tears welling up in my eyes. He said: "Don't worry, let's meet next week and talk."

As he walked away, ready to make his end-of-year speech to a packed audience, I felt angry and embarrassed at the way I had reacted. How was I able to keep it together each day in the office surrounded by my colleagues and yet now, in front of the grand fromage, of all people, I had completely lost it! Making my way to the Tube, my emotions frozen by the icy weather, I had a realisation. The fact that the man in power that evening took the time to search for me in a crowded room, ask me how I was feeling and deal with my burst of emotion in a kind and thoughtful way, caught me off guard. He made me feel that, like him, I was a "somebody" in that room and that my feelings mattered.

Imran Sheikh is another man I would mention here. Asked by our CEO to co-chair the organisation's ethnic minorities network in the UK, Imran and I worked hard to turn this network into a positive and energetic force for good, trebling members and winning industry awards. Not only did I learn so much from this man in power, but I also started to rediscover my own voice.

"Why do you hold back on certain topics?" was one of the first questions Imran asked me. The reason I kept my thoughts to myself was because around that time, a colleague close to the top of the tree had described me to others – though not to my face – as someone "lacking in interpersonal skills." This was a first for me! This brutal description of me to those who didn't know me well hit me hard and I stupidly chose to believe it to be true. Otherwise, I reasoned to myself, why on earth would she say that about me? I have written a whole chapter about this type of behaviour in the workplace, so I will not go into it here. Suffice to say that over time, her frosty words melted away as the flame of my confidence grew stronger.

Imran repeatedly neutralised the pain of these harsh words, encouraging me to really say what was on my mind, knowing that it would provoke thought in others and help steer us in the right direction. His encouragement culminated in forcing me, once again, to step outside my comfort zone.

I had been working with The Circle NGO, founded by the great Annie Lennox OBE. She had very kindly agreed to be interviewed as part of a panel event at our Canary Wharf offices, to help raise awareness for her charity's initiatives. Imran's words were point blank: "You must interview her. You are the only one who can do it." That could not possibly be true! How could I get out of it? But I couldn't … and I'm so glad I didn't. As nerve-wracking as this was, sharing a stage with an extraordinarily impressive panel in front of an audience of one hundred people, I had the time of my life and found myself enjoying every second of it!

Just as Rupert Bondy recognised my feelings as being important, Imran convinced me that my voice was, too, and that it could be used as a force for positive change. Many years have passed since then, but I continue to seek the wise counsel of these and other men – and women! – whom I trust and respect. Their empathy, authentic leadership and constant encouragement have allowed me to dream big and intentionally use my voice to help others.

As Elvis explained: ***"It's not how much you have that makes people look up to you, it's who you are."***

Journal

Journal

Chapter 7

ALWAYS TAKE THE STAIRS

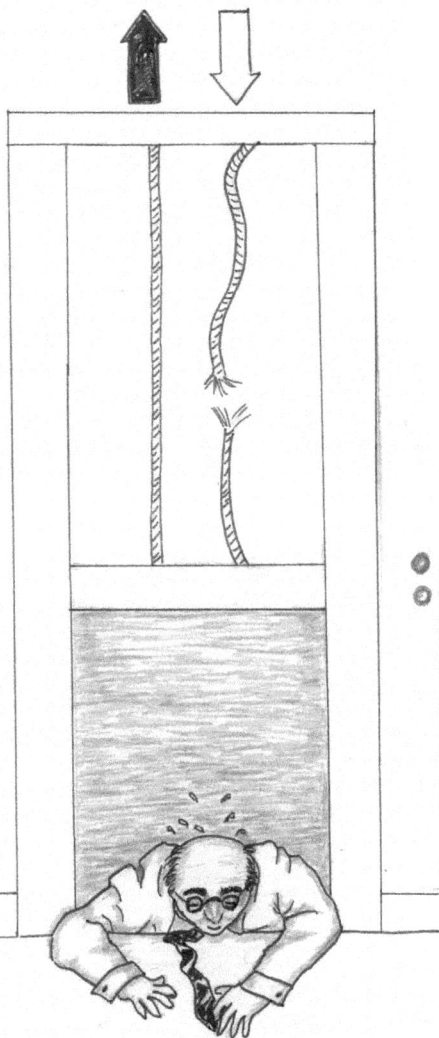

We all know that inserting moments of physical exertion into our daily lives, particularly when we're sat at a desk for most of the time, is a good thing. Those wanting to watch their weight will smugly tell you "I took the stairs!", while holding back gulps of breath, to demonstrate their health, vitality and sheer willpower. Good for them, provided that in a pandemic-ridden world they are not breathing too heavily near you!

I, on the other hand, prefer to think about this concept from a mental well-being perspective. Of course, shedding excess weight when needed is healthy for our physical body, but I think the idea of shedding excess weight to lighten our mental state is more vital. Each of you reading this will, like me, no doubt have faced knock-backs and disappointments, either in your personal lives or your professional careers. That is part of the rich weave of life's tapestry, as the saying goes. Sure, these experiences are never pleasant at the time and in some cases these unpleasant feelings can continue in varying degrees for days, weeks, months, basically as long as we will let them. However, what I want us to focus on here is how we can pull ourselves out of this dip, strengthen ourselves for the next step or, if you like, the next more colourful section of that tapestry.

Let's face it, knock-backs are tough, full stop. Whether it's the partner you could imagine blissfully living the rest of your life with who suddenly decides you're not the one for them, or the promotion you had set your sights on, knowing that you were the best candidate for the role, but for whatever reason or bias (conscious or unconscious), things didn't work out the way you had hoped. It's downright painful to deal with. That's OK, and in fact completely normal. I always think that feeling hurt simply means you care, and no matter how much you try it is hard to pretend otherwise. So, accept those initial feelings of shock, rejection, disappointment, betrayal, anger and frustration, knowing that psychologically and chemically, they are temporary. As Eckhart Tolle explains in his inspiring book, *The Power of Now: A Guide to Spiritual Enlightenment*, this is purely the "pain-body" being triggered. We all experience this because we are human.

However, what I find interesting is that this pain-body or form of energy which thrives on emotional pain, really is a temporary feeling. Neurologically, emotions last in our bodies for a mere ninety seconds. That's it. What keeps us in a state of pain-body is our constant playback of the event in our minds. Simply put, if you keep playing the same scene, it will register more intensely in your mind and trick you into feeling those emotions over and over again. And for what purpose? Psychologists refer to this as "rumination". I think of it as a form of self-sabotage. Put bluntly, a vicious cycle of addiction to unhappiness and even victimhood. Now, I am not suggesting for one minute that we somehow switch off our feelings after the initial ninety seconds: that is not humanly possible for most of us. What I am suggesting, though, is that we start to recognise these mental playbacks, observe them as an innocent bystander, watching without judging, recognising what is happening and allowing ourselves the choice (and it really is a choice) to free ourselves of these constraining acts. We know that going over the past doesn't change it, but what we can change is how we react in the present. This is the focus I would now like to switch to.

Let's go back to that smug co-worker who took the stairs. We can even give him a name: Victor – I know the hidden meaning won't be lost on you! Physically, he has put in the effort, literally step by step, to reach the floor he aimed for. Yes, he could have taken the lift, but where's the fun in that when no effort is involved? Victor might even have decided that he would rather not be cooped up in a restricted space with several others, who may potentially have negative viewpoints, which may impact his way of thinking and with whom, at worst, he might get stuck, going nowhere, possibly resulting in him missing his meeting altogether. OK, I accept that this way of thinking could be viewed as catastrophising, but for the sake of the analogy I am attempting to create here, please may I ask that you suspend your disbelief with me just for a little longer! In choosing to take the stairs, Victor really has demonstrated his willpower. Rather like an athlete who chooses not to take the easy route, but instead to challenge herself by rigorous training, day in and day out, conquering fears and injuries, as well as her own and others' disbelief in her strength and abilities. All of this to allow herself the possibility of winning.

So, what's my point with all of this? Well, let's flip back to the mental analogy. We can all accept that setbacks and disappointments are a hurdle. They are bumps in the road leading you from A to B. We each have the choice to either avoid a hurdle, which is often out of our control, or to look at it *ad infinitum* and continue feeling angry or frustrated, stuck in the same position and powerless to move on from misdirecting our energy and emotions. Or, like the athlete, we can choose another way: a more challenging way, but a more rewarding one. We can train our thoughts every day by recognising negative patterns, watching them as the innocent bystander and choosing to give them no importance, instead replacing them with positive, compassionate and constructive beliefs.

I appreciate that initially, at least, this is certainly not the easy route. As we know, the brain is also a muscle that needs training in order to be strengthened, so that this strength can allow it to perform efficiently and clearly. Just as taking the stairs requires effort so, too, does consciously rewiring our thought processes and forcing ourselves to do things differently, until it becomes second nature. With this endurance and willpower, each stair raises us higher and once we start to climb, our destination becomes closer and clearer, so that finally, we can stand at the top of the stairs, look down and feel proud of how far we have come. That is achievement. That is winning. With all this in-built strength, it is harder to become lazy, to be tempted back into the lift, to press "ground" and to hit the bottom again but this time quicker and sometimes harder.

In an uncertain world, particularly the one in which we all currently live, one of the things that is certain is that setbacks will happen, but what you can also be certain of is that it is often these very setbacks which will lead you to your ultimate success, through conscious training … one step at a time.

Journal

Journal

Chapter 8

EMPLOYEES NEED SPACE

t was July. Cerulean blue skies, puffs of white clouds and the leaves of the plane trees outside my office window were glistening in the warmth of the summer sun. But there was a weight like thick drapery hanging over me.

My phone rang. I heard the tone of her voice and I knew. He was gone.

Even writing these words causes my chest to swell a little, tears gently filling my eyes. We had lost him at 28. The Oxford Blue (several times over), the smartest guy who managed approximately one hour of work during his entire four years at university and still topped the highest exam grade that year in one of his finals papers on Logic. He was too busy smashing sports records on the rackets and real tennis courts, beating every single opponent and still finding time to make me laugh so hysterically as he pretended to chat up the cold marble female busts along the corridor of the library, where I was trying desperately to prepare for my next essay. Where it was so cold one night that he ran over to his room to get his gloves; one for each of us so that whilst we were writing, our other hand could be warm. He was left-handed, I was right-handed. Logic. The guy who, six foot tall, would spontaneously lift me upside down, so that I could get a different perspective on things. Who would sit up through the night with me on several occasions to tell me that one boy or another who had hurt my feelings was not worth my tears and then with only a couple of hours to get home and sleep, would be off to play a cricket match miles away. My friend, Alex.

He was young and healthy, with so much to give. Hit by a car whose driver was over the alcohol limit and sped off leaving my friend to fight for his life.

I am sure we have all lost someone dear to us. It hurts. It really hurts. Hearing the shocking news in the office, in an environment where long hours and machismo were key to success, where my boss at the time, on hearing the news, suggested that I sit in a data room filled with stale lever arch folders and carry out some corporate due diligence for a large power project, to take my mind off things. This was his idea of support. I couldn't quite believe this display of so-called leadership.

So, how can we support colleagues in their tougher times, in particular when dealing with grief or any other loss? As with most things, the answer lies in empathy. Work is important, but life in its fullest sense is what we are here to experience. From my own perspective, the offer of space, time away from the office, emails and meetings is important to be able to start to process things in a healthy way, without the distractions of work or other unnecessary pressures. However, this offer of space needs to be genuine, and by that I mean offered in such a way, that it does not leave the employee feeling that they owe the company something, nor that they are being clock-watched as to how long they will need. Especially when business is busy and people are already feeling stretched.

I have spoken with colleagues who worry what others might be thinking, wondering whether they are being regarded as "soft" or "weak". These concerns can easily be shifted from minds which are already dealing with raw emotions by employers managing each circumstance with sensitivity, respect and care. This all sounds remarkably obvious, I know, but how many of us have been disappointed by the actions and reactions of those who should know better, being in a position of power and supposedly, trust?

Employees are owed this time to take care of themselves and those around them, to deal with unpleasant duties, forms and processes, and to have a chance to focus on what they need in times of deep pain. In return, the employer will often find they are able to welcome back a colleague who has been given this space to work through what they need to, or at least to begin the process, with a slightly clearer head and hopefully with a little more energy and motivation.

Grief takes time. The pain of losing someone never diminishes, our inner strength just grows around it and we teach ourselves how to cope. Memories stay alive, sometimes to make us contemplative and sometimes to remind us how lucky we were to have that person in our lives.

Alex, we miss you. Thank you for being my friend.

Journal

Journal

Chapter 9

THE POWER
OF PAINT

am an aesthete, I admit it. Beauty, symmetry, music and art in general have always been some of my strongest passions. So strong, in fact, that a colour scheme, a piece of music or someone's faultless harmony can really brighten my mood in seconds.

What I look like can also have a huge impact on how I feel that day. I know it is probably stating the obvious that walking out of the house in a pair of sweatpants, a baggy jumper and with no makeup on is not necessarily going to lift anyone's mood, unless of course you are dressed this way because you are soon to be transformed by a glam squad, or heading to a spa for a restorative treatment. Most of us don't live the Beverley Hills lifestyle, so when we are dressed this way we are really just dropping the children off at school, putting out the bins or making a quick dash to the corner shop for emergency supplies.

Now, I am not trying to suggest that getting dressed up and slapping on makeup is what we should all be aiming for in order to feel cheered up. Nor am I suggesting that our ultimate aim should be to reflect the striking looks of the '90s supermodels in order to feel good about ourselves – although it would help! What I am trying to suggest is a way of creating a sense of inner strength and optimism from our everyday 'look'. Crazy, some of you might say, or even frivolous. But I disagree. This sense of the outside mirroring the inside, the link between mind and body, has been around for centuries.

The Romans knew this only too well: *"mens sana in corpore sano"* or, to put it in plain English, "a healthy mind in a healthy body". Psychologists will tell you the two are very much connected. Anxiety, for example, can create inexplicable physical ailments such as stomach pains, backache and dizziness, whereas depression often leaves the sufferer bereft of energy, motivation and ultimately joy. If we feel good mentally, we tend to radiate a healthy glow and feel more compelled to get out, exercise and look after ourselves and others.

Let's focus here on the face, as the impact of a well-tailored outfit and heels deserve a chapter all of its own. I strongly believe in the power of makeup. Sure, when applied it physically transforms the wearer for better or worse, depending on how well it is applied! But more than this, I firmly believe that it has a deeper, psychological impact on the wearer. Makeup is not a mask. It is an enhancer, an amplifier of our features, expressions and feelings. Applied well, it displays the best version of ourselves in every way.

Early on in my career, I seriously considered ditching my day job as a private practice lawyer in the City, swapping my work with black and white printed documents for the splashes and swirls of colour as a makeup artist. I took an evening course at the Delamar Academy, based at Ealing Studios, and would ease myself into blissful sleep after a long day, thinking of colour wheels, bone structure and artistic creations which I would practise on myself and willing friends and family. I can't remember if it was the reality of 2 am starts on film sets, the long and gruelling hours spent mostly standing and bending in awkward positions to transform my client, or the stark numbers I needed to earn to pay my large mortgage and bills which guided me away from this career change. But I suppose at the core of my decision to remain in law was that I was simply not dedicated enough to truly want to pursue a career as a makeup artist.

It nonetheless taught me so much about the joy of application and transformation, and how both of these have the effect of enhancing my mood. I was also privileged enough to watch how the power of makeup lifted the mood of patients undergoing chemotherapy and radiotherapy, when volunteering as a makeup artist for the fantastic charity Look Good Feel Better. Focussing on the face and learning about application techniques, colours, shading and brightening caused these patients to temporarily forget about what they were going through medically and to treat themselves as the person they remembered, watching their familiar self slowly smiling back at them in the mirror.

And for those men whom I may well have lost by this stage, makeup is not just a "woman's issue". In fact, traced back over 7,000 years, makeup was originally worn by men to appeal to the gods. Indigenous tribes continue to wear face paint as part of their culture. To this day, the men of Chad's nomadic Wodaabe tribe, also known as "the vainest tribe in the world", continue to wear makeup and pay close attention to their hair and wardrobe. They would certainly give Boy George a run for his money!

Although a couple of my previous boyfriends were keen on the "no makeup, makeup look" or, ideally, none at all, I had to explain to them that I was not wearing makeup for their benefit. I continue to wear makeup for me and me alone, as do most women (and men). The simple act of cleansing, moisturising and applying thin layers of colour over my face has really been my favourite form of a mindfulness exercise. Whether I am doing this first thing in the morning or before an evening out, it pushes me to take a good look in the mirror and start to like and accept what stares back at me. Eat your heart out, Cindy, Christy, Naomi and Linda!

The COVID-19 pandemic taught us many things, central to which is the importance of our physical and mental wellbeing. So, how have we emerged from this surreal existence? Likening that pandemic to the Spanish Flu, some theorists predicted a return to something similar to the Roaring Twenties, ushering in fresh, brave and risqué fashions, bright colours, shorter hemlines and new dance crazes and resulting in the Jazz Age. Others predicted a return to more basic and essential trends, toned-down and neutral looks using sustainable materials, all in support of nurturing rather than burning our planet, particularly with growing concerns around climate change. What we have witnessed is a combination of these two theories: an injection of colour, texture and joy, alongside comfort, nostalgia and purposeful environmental awareness.

Garish or subdued, one thing remains the same: makeup can be used creatively to express ourselves and to enhance our mental well-being, but only if we want it to.

The much-admired makeup artist Lisa Eldridge articulates this beautifully in her book *Face Paint: The Story of Makeup*: *"I love the fact that you can conceal a temporary blemish on your chin and immediately feel more confident – a touch of blush to feel healthier and a coat of mascara to look and feel wide awake ... Ultimately, nothing empowers a woman more than the right to a good education, and the freedom to choose whether to wear a red lip and smokey eye ... or not."* I powerfully agree!

Journal

Journal

Chapter 10

FOLLOW THE RAINBOW OR THE CONCRETE ROAD?

think we are all familiar with *The Wizard of Oz*, released in Technicolor in 1939. It starred a teenage Judy Garland as the protagonist, Dorothy, who was pushed (literally) into an unfamiliar world, following a cyclone that hit her hometown in Kansas, USA. As you know, along her journey she meets the Scarecrow (representing low self-esteem), the Tin Man (representing repressed emotions) and the Cowardly Lion (representing anxiety). The thread running throughout the movie is Dorothy's quest to return home, whilst experiencing fantastical situations and characters along the way.

Since its release there has been much debate about the true meaning behind the movie, ranging from political dichotomies to psychological and spiritual insights. What I want to explore here, though, is this sense of home and the yearning to return – not because your commute or the weather have been abhorrent, but because of something a little more profound – the need to return to the real you.

If we cast our minds back over the past few decades, the entertainment industry has shone its ethereal light on countless individuals shining like stars over the humdrum, the quotidian, the ordinary – us. Each of these stellar personas appeared to encapsulate the ultimate dream – beauty, fame and money. Their onscreen lives were meticulously mapped out, their diets regimentally scheduled and their personal lives, in the most part, hidden from our "normal" lives. There are so many examples: Rock Hudson's homosexuality carefully concealed to ensure his male lead roles were believable, and his female fans still struck with the hope of winning his heart one day; Doris Day's white picket fence characters covering up the reality of a turbulent marriage, putting up with a husband who gambled away her hard graft and the fruit of her talents; or Loretta Young, who carried the secret of giving birth to Clarke Gable's daughter, going as far as covering her toddler's head with hats and bonnets so as not to have her father's characteristically large ears on display to the prying public, instead allowing them to believe that her little girl was adopted.

Arguably the most traumatic outcome of showbusiness' attempts to hide the reality of many of its creations is the scale of addiction, substance abuse and mental exhaustion, even breakdowns experienced by some of the hugest talents. In some cases, this burnout is as a result of constant pressure to be or to do something not truly reflecting their inner attributes. In short, they are proactively starved of their creativity – the oxygen to their wellness and joy. Greedy managers and talentless hangers-on, puffing up their own self-worth by sucking the souls out of their ever-fragile circus act. I need only mention Baz Luhrmann's much-acclaimed biographical film *Elvis* as just one depiction of how unearthly talent was relentlessly squeezed dry to fill Colonel Tom Parker's pockets. Sure, Elvis benefitted financially too, but often at the expense of having the freedom to do what he really wanted. How many beautiful musical arrangements and heart-rending ballads would we have enjoyed if Elvis had been allowed the freedom to shape his own, very individual creativity? Not just here and there, but throughout his career?

So where am I going with all of this?

Well, bringing it into the corporate world, I have watched hugely talented employees slowly having their bright and enthusiastic feathers plucked out, one by one. Whether this is due to a lack of challenging work, a bad boss, a ruthless leader, toxic office politics, workplace envy or a looming round of lay-offs, each drop of negativity drip-feeds its way into an increasingly tired, demotivated and sceptical individual, gradually wearing away at the Technicolor within them, leaving them with only grey, hard, lifeless concrete. In time, the Scarecrow, the Tin Man and the Cowardly Lion all make an appearance to a greater or lesser extent, symbolising low self-esteem, repressed emotions and anxiety, all played out along a grey, concrete road.

As my experience increased over time, I felt more able to step in early on in the cycle and provide support and encouragement to some of these individuals whom I felt could do with an empathetic ear and often a shoulder to cry on, in an attempt to re-boot the picture, correct the colour and adjust the lighting.

Here are some of the tools I have shared with them to reframe the display screen:

- **Write a list of what you are proud of in your life** – it could be an award you have received, a tough deal you have successfully completed, a new country or culture you have assimilated into, family commitments you have sustained, friendships you have nurtured – whatever it is, write it down and read it, often.
- **Return to happy memories** – recall the times when you felt the most relaxed, joyous and content, and have a think about why those situations made you feel good.
- **What makes you tick** – when do you, or those closest to you, notice a resurgence of energy, a lightness about you, or even a glittering twinkle in your eye in both your professional and your personal life?
- **Get yourself a good mentor or coach** – perhaps this is someone with whom you have already worked, someone in your wider network, a professional who comes recommended, a family friend. If you can, pick a few, each covering specific aspects of your career – some refer to this as creating your own personal boardroom. I really like that idea.

- **Stay alert** – keep your finger on the market pulse for new employment opportunities, networking events, industry groups you can join or individual connections you can make to broaden your experience and perspectives.
- **Look for other ways you can beef up your skills** – within your organisation by joining committees or professional networks, and outside your organisation by considering, for example, board roles or volunteering opportunities.
- **Assemble your cheerleaders** – surround yourself with those who you know have your best interests at heart, who listen to and support you during both the ups and the downs, and who offer considered and wise advice.
- **Make space for doing what you enjoy** – this may sound obvious, but how often do we feel we have the time to indulge in the activities or hobbies which bring us peace of mind? Yet these are some of the most important diary events we can schedule to ensure our overall well-being, helping to balance out the grey with Technicolor.

Going back to Judy Garland, a hugely talented child star forced into addiction by the studios handing her the equivalent of what we know in the modern-day as speed, to get her through the gruelling filming agenda of *The Wizard of Oz*. Her career had its ups and downs. Controlled by the studios, she definitely encountered real-life Scarecrow, Tin Man and Cowardly Lion emotions, but still she poured her heart into her performances, belting out legendary ballads, singing to packed music halls and studio audiences, all the while continuing the only way she knew how, through addiction. Another entertainment legend summed it up perfectly:

"Every time she sings, she dies a little. That's how much she gives." (Frank Sinatra on Judy Garland)

Chapter 11

THE SHOW MUST GO ON

They say confidence is silent and insecurity is loud.

You need only look at some of the best-loved artists to notice a striking common denominator: many of them are natural introverts. They pack stadiums, theatres and cinemas with adoring fans, their faces lit up by glaring stage and studio lights. They tolerate the requisite lightning flashes of paparazzi mobs, all with one aim in mind: getting that multi-million-dollar photo, which can be beamed across our newspapers, screens and billboards to satisfy the Zeitgeist. All this should be the very last thing these self-identified reserved types should want to do for a living. Yet they do. They seem to be drawn to the opposing side of their beings, either by stepping into an alter ego or a scripted character and performing, loud and proud. It is almost as if something outside their very introversion pulls them out of their comfort zone and into the spotlight, even if only for a relatively short time.

Many performers admit to having stage fright right before the curtain rises, or the cameras roll, fearing they will fluff their lines, forget the lyrics, chords or carefully crafted choreography. But they go out there, believing, as Freddie Mercury would tell us, that The Show Must Go On.

Insecurity is usually fear-based. Performers who face their fears, often go on to exceed their goals, working through their fear, by training, learning and better understanding themselves.

Insecurity can therefore be a good thing – it had better be, since each one of us has it, to a greater or lesser extent. The issue is how we choose to use it or, rather, to work with it.

Since I like to end on a positive note, let's start with the ugly side of insecurity: the one that overtakes a person's behaviour, causing them to actively harm another purely to make themselves feel better. Here are some of the more blatant ways this can play out in the professional arena:

- **The Slammer** – the person who doesn't think twice about shutting down or silencing someone's voice in a meeting. Now don't get me wrong: I am all for the efficient use of people's time, but remarks such as: "That point has already been made", when it hasn't, or brushing aside a legitimate question or concern raised in a meeting, are all micro-aggressions used to belittle and ultimately, knock the confidence out of someone, with the aim of silencing them – extinguishing their voice.
- **The Under-Carpet Sweeper** – choosing to ignore a colleague's achievements, industry awards and accolades is a tactic that can be used to try to turn down the amplifier to zero, reducing another's oxygen, and can ultimately stunt their professional growth. Deliberate amplification of the achievements of a select few, namely "favourites" (see The Targeter, below) is a common detraction.
- **The Gossip Denier** – the one who says they don't gossip, but whom others will eventually learn not to trust because of what they say about others, and who they say it to. The aim here is to undermine someone who may be achieving more by placing doubt in others' minds about their motivations, all based on falsehoods, massaging of the truth or strategic miscommunication. This is a stealth play that often backfires once the truth is unearthed. The Gossip Denier often believes they are outwitting their opponents, but what they don't realise is that in time, their clandestine ways always come up to the surface for all to view.
- **The Propagandist** – this is the slow drip-feed of malicious mischaracterisation of a perceived opponent to someone of importance within an organisation. Describing a colleague as "lacking in social skills", when in fact the opposite is true, is one example of how this can play out. Here, the hope is

that the message will spread in a strategic way, ensuring that the right people speak to the right people to propagate the damaging myth.

- **The Targeter** – these are the ones who create lists of targets to take down. The victims in these cases are identified as perceived threats, rightly or wrongly. The Targeter will build a portfolio of negatives around the target and use other tools to try to ensure their careers go nowhere, or at least make them pay by waiting longer for their professional rewards. Meritocracy is not an important factor here. The Targeter creates a like-minded court around them to ensure there is no challenge within that echo chamber.
- **The Mother-Seller** – in some ways, this one underlies all types of dangerous individuals. In other words, they have no comprehension of a moral code and will do whatever it takes to get ahead, whether that's failing to advocate for someone when they are not in the room, or making promises they have no intention of keeping, or failing to promote on merit, but instead relying on cultivated friendships or a fear of skeletons being let out of closets. You get the picture.

In contrast, though, if you are someone who is fully aware of your insecurities and fears (these may be in the form of negative self-talk, self-comparisons or envy), but you don't allow them to overpower you and instead use them as an inbuilt learning tool to notice your triggers, and work to overcome them, this will not only grow your resilience but will also reduce those insecurities and fears on both a personal and professional level, so that in time, they are 'less loud' and out of the artificial spotlight.

Below are some methods which may be helpful in working through these concerns and diminishing the power of that insecurity or fear.

(i)   <u>Acceptance</u> – this is perhaps the hardest step, but it is the first step on the road to recovery. Really take an honest look at your insecurities and fears and actively decide to do something about them in order to have a more fulfilling career.

(ii)   <u>Focus on the areas you find trickier</u> – this might be the numbers, analysing spreadsheets, reading contracts more thoroughly, making presentations, or networking. Whatever it is, really spend dedicated time to strengthen those weaknesses as best you can.

(iii)   <u>Seek regular feedback</u> – from trusted individuals, to help steer you towards the true light within yourself (rather than the stage lights). This can also be a valuable way of receiving constructive feedback and working on clearly defined areas.

(iv)   <u>Coaching</u> – either personal or professional, to gain a degree of objectivity and perspective with the aid of a trained adviser.

(v)   <u>Trust the process</u> – being comfortable that the course may be bumpy, but showing yourself compassion along the way and taking each day at a time can help to limit those more anxious moments.

(vi)   <u>Celebrate the wins</u> – take the time to congratulate yourself, no matter the size of the wins. Each is a stepping stone to being your true and better self.

I started with Freddie Mercury, so perhaps I should let him have the last word on this:

*"**You can be anything you want to be, just turn yourself into anything you think that you could ever be.**"* (Freddie Mercury)

Journal

Journal

Chapter 12

CAN YOU LOOK YOURSELF IN THE MIRROR?

"No matter how tempting the deal, make sure you can still look yourself in the mirror."

These were the wise words shared with a respected oil trader in the industry as she embarked on her career at an international organisation. Yes, you read it correctly: "she". This incredibly intelligent woman not only made millions of dollars for that organisation, but also managed to do it looking as though she had stepped off the catwalk from Paris Fashion Week, nonchalantly advertising the latest haute couture collection (often the sophisticated monochrome of Chanel, for those who are interested) to a sea of mostly men sitting at white desks that held up black screens flashing with numbers in red and green.

In my first week in that same organisation, her elegant yet purposeful stride down the trading floor to my desk, her voice already audible several metres away, above the threatening sound of sharp voices amplified through the daily squawk box from Singapore, and the sparkle in her brown eyes as she began to talk me through one particular deal, told me that she meant business. She had a dilemma on her hands and wanted to speak to a lawyer who could help. Knowingly sailing close to the wind, she was adamant that she wanted to remain on the right side of the law. I heard her out, understood the challenge she was facing and knew she was in cleaner waters than she suspected. "Let me help you sort this out" were the words I offered to this doyenne sitting opposite me. From that moment on, I had her trust and she had mine.

Years later, she explained why: "You were the first lawyer I spoke to who was able to clearly separate the legal and regulatory exposure from the commercial exposure and potential reputational risk. You helped me navigate the grey areas. Very few things we do in trading are as simple as black and white. Mostly, they are grey. You could explain the white (being the legal and regulatory framework), discuss the grey and steer me away from the black in my commercial decision-making."

As a lawyer very much used to the bravado and brawl on a trading floor, supporting hundreds of traders, business originators, financial structurers and the like, I felt it was my responsibility to keep them in the cleaner waters. Now by this I don't mean that they were particularly looking for trouble: as we all know, there are certain deals which appear bright and inviting on the outside, rather like a golden apple. Take one bite and you know pretty quickly whether its promise of sweetness materialises, or whether it shocks by stinging the tongue. These type of deals appear highly lucrative at the outset, almost too good to be true and sure enough, their cheap veneer is often quickly scratched, cracking indiscriminately across the polished surface to reveal a mottled and decaying core.

There are those who actively look for the loopholes, who do business by scrapping and scraping at the edges to make a quick buck, indifferent to any legal restrictions, let alone principles. Those are not the traders or commercial teams I know and respect. The best of them are the ones who know when to speak to their lawyers, who listen (even when they do not like the advice) and who respect professional boundaries. The most successful traders don't just trade an asset (whether it be commodities, equities or a financial underlying), they trade on their reputation. The more you are prepared to swim in the black, the less likely you are to be relied on as a counterpart long-term.

This idea of being able to look yourself in the mirror is clearly subjective. But for me, it's not just about being able to look at yourself: more importantly, it's about liking what you see. I don't necessarily mean aesthetically – although, as they say, beauty is in the eye of the beholder! For those of you old enough to remember the American sitcom *Happy Days*, its protagonist, The Fonz, springs to mind in his jeans and black leather jacket covering a crisp white cotton T-shirt, looking admiringly in the mirror for a couple of seconds before realising that the reflection was, to him at least, perfection. Rather, by liking what you see in your reflection, I mean this in an ethical sense.

For some who have been navigating the grey for so long that they sail deeper and deeper into it, making it almost impossible to discern the dark grey from the black, ethical lines have already started to blur. Sometimes this is intentional. More often than not, though, it is a result of small and often subtle shifts in moving the goalposts, to such an extent that the ethical lines completely disappear. To put it another way, the moral compass has broken and it is usually too late or too difficult to sail back to a safe berth. They have not taken the time to pause, breathe and take a step back to look at themselves in the mirror. Some companies choose to operate in this way, conditioning their employees to keep sailing without planning for storms, sharks and pirates. As we know, corporate culture plays such an important part, not just in the way that companies do business, but also in the profound impact it can have on its people.

There are, however, others who, like me, have worked for decades in the grey, analysing its fifty shades (sorry, I couldn't help myself!) and collaborating closely with their commercial teams to steer clear of the darker waters. It is these lawyers who are energised by the intellect of their commercial counterparts, buoyed up on a daily basis in the knowledge that they are adding to the success of the businesses they support and ensuring they continue to sail through the cleaner waters.

These are the lawyers who are able to look in the mirror, head held high, sometimes exhausted, but always clear that they can look at the reflection, even take a step back and still like what they see. Happy days, indeed.

Journal

Journal

THE HOPE

I hope that you have enjoyed this companion as much as I have enjoyed putting each chapter and illustration together for you.

I hope that you continue to use this as a point of reference, perhaps even as a guide to remind you that no matter what the situation, you have all the tools to deal with it in grace, positivity and hope.

Thank you for spending time with me.

I hope for the very best for you.